Cal Naps a Bit

by Brooke Kelly
illustrated by Arun Lee

Practice Decodable 5

McGraw Hill Education

Bothell, WA • Chicago, IL • Columbus, OH • New York, NY

MHEonline.com

Send all inquiries to:
McGraw-Hill Education
8787 Orion Place
Columbus, OH 43240

ISBN: 978-0-02-145028-2
MHID: 0-02-145028-5

Printed in China.

9 10 11 12 13 DSS 27 26 25 24 23

Cal is a cat.

Cal can nap a bit.

His pal is Tab.

His pal is in a cat band.

Bam! Bam! Bam! Bam!

Can Cal nap?